Successfu

Secrets

Book Marketing Tips From a BestMake YOU a Book Marketing Hero

Daniel Mason

TABLE OF CONTENT

INTRODUCTION

Welcome to the **Successful Book Launch Secrets**. You're about to learn **Book Marketing Tips From a Bestselling Author to Make YOU a Book Marketing Hero**. In this book, I'm going to share with you what I've learned in the process of launching thirty Christian books that have sold more than 1.5 million copies around the world.

Let's face it, if you've gone to all the trouble of writing a book – *or if you are in the process of writing one* –you want people to actually read it. That's the whole idea. If you were writing for your own amusement and edification, you wouldn't be publishing.

But since you are choosing either to self-publish or partner with a traditional publishing house, it's safe to assume your goal is to reach as many readers as possible.

I'm here to help.

Now, there are lots of people who will *claim* that they can tell you how to sell lots of books. But I will let you in on a little secret: most of them have never sold more than a few thousand copies of their own books. And some haven't even sold a few hundred copies. I know, because I have software that shows me the real numbers.

I promise not to spend this book *tooting my own horn* and talking about myself. *BORING!* But I do think it's important for you to know that launching successful books is something I've worked very hard at for three decades. Not *three years.* Three decades.

My thirty books have been consistent bestsellers, ranging from 35,000 to 75,000 (solid bestsellers) to 150,000 and even 300,000 (pretty phenomenal). To put that in context, the average self-published book sells around 100 copies; the average traditionally-published Christian book sells less than 1,000 copies.

In the interest of full-disclosure, I should also admit: I've had a few books that didn't sell well. *And one or two of them totally bombed.* (And by bombed, I mean they sold about 5,000 copies.) I learned some very hard lessons as a result. The great thing is: you can learn from both my successes and my failures – because I share about both very honestly throughout **The Christian Author's Guide Series**.

I'm assuming that most people reading this series are pursuing self-publishing on Amazon KDP, with a view to expanding onto other distribution platforms later. In today's publishing environment, I think that's the smart way to go. Once you've proven yourself and established yourself as an authority, you'll be much better positioned to pursue a traditional book deal.

However, there are plenty of tips here for those who are on the traditional publishing track.

There are pros and cons to both approaches. And I know that from personal experience. That's why I've chosen to be a Hybrid Author. That means I've rejected the typical either-or framework. Instead, I think you can and *should* publish both ways.

The vast majority of my books (28) are traditionally-published; but I'm enjoying increasing success with my self-published books and am in the process of rapidly expanding in that market.

Typically, it works the other way. You begin by self-publishing. Learn how to do it right and build up a great track record. Then, from that strong position, you can approach a traditional publishing house for future book projects.

One important caveat: it's almost impossible to convince a traditional publisher to republish a book you've self-published. So as you are writing, be sure to consider: which approach is best for *this* particular book?

For the most part, my devotionals and bible studies are better-suited to a broad market, so traditional publishing is the smart choice for those. But for a niche book, like those featured in **The Christian Author's Guide Series**, self-publishing just makes more sense.

So are you ready to discover all of my *Successful Book Launch Secrets*? If so, it's time to dive into the wonderful world of marketing.

Did that word just scare you? Does marketing sound unspiritual? Can't we just write what God puts on our hearts then pray the Holy Spirit will tell everyone to go buy the book?

Yes and no.

Yes, we should write what God puts on our hearts.

Yes, we should pray that the Holy Spirit will prompt people to buy our books. In fact, I pray that all the time. And after 30 years in this industry, I can tell you for sure: the Holy Spirit is the best public relations agent and the best book marketing expert EVER.

And yes, I give God all the glory for the miraculous ways my books have reached people around the world.

But no, it's not enough to say a prayer and hope for the best.

We have to pray hard…and work smart.

So let's get back to that scary word "marketing" and talk about what it actually means.   Marketing is simply *letting people know all about you, your book and how you can help them.* That's it!

That doesn't sound too scary and unspiritual, does it? Good, now that we are on the same page and clear about our goal, the rest of this book will walk you through the process of positioning yourself for the most successful book launch possible.

We will cover this together in 10 Steps.

10 STEPS TO A
SUCCESSFUL BOOK LAUNCH
The Can't-Fail Blueprint for Christian Authors

1	2	3	4	5
MINDSET	**CREATE**	**CLARIFY**	**BUILD**	**CAPTURE**
Develop a Marketing Mindset	Your Super Hero Identity	Who You Are Talking To	A Loyal Tribe of People	Attention with Your Book Description

6	7	8	9	10
PROVE	**MOJO**	**INVEST**	**ENGAGE**	**WRITE**
Show Social Proof to Potential Buyers	Build Momentum through Free or .99 Promotion	Consider Paid Book Promotion To Continue Momentum	Stay Active on Social Media	Write Another Book, Amazon Loves Series!

STEP 1: DEVELOP A MARKETING MINDSET

YOU ARE GOD'S MESSENGER

If you're reading this, it's because you are a Christian. And you have a message that's been burning in your heart. Now, you are finally ready to TAKE YOUR MESSAGE TO THE WORLD.

That's why I want to teach you some marketing strategies (oh no! there's that terrifying, unspiritual word again!!!) that will enable you to have a Successful Book Launch. Our goal together will be position you to reach as many readers as you possibly can.

Let's make an agreement, okay? I'm convinced it will help you forever after. Here it is. From now on, whenever you hear the word marketing, just think **message**.

Because that's all marketing is: it's getting your message out there. It's letting your voice be heard. Suddenly, it doesn't sound so unspiritual, right?

I want you to keep in mind three key points:

1. You are a messenger.
2. People need your message.
3. People must believe the messenger or they won't receive the message.

This is especially true with a non-fiction book. People typically have to buy in to the messenger before they'll buy the book.

If your goal is to transform lives with your message, then your book should really just be a foundation upon which you build. Ideally, it should be a way to introduce readers to you and your message, so that you can invite them into a deeper relationship with you.

YOUR MARKETING MINDSET

Here is your new Marketing Mindset in a nutshell:

- Marketing is telling the people who have a problem about the solution you have found.

- If you believe in the answers you've found, why wouldn't you tell as many people as possible, in every way possible?

- If you don't have answers, don't write a book.

- If you do have answers *(and I know you do!)*, write your book. Then market it with everything you've got.

BEYOND THE BOOK

If the goal of your book is to change lives, then let me strongly encourage you to prayerfully consider going Beyond the Book. By that, I mean providing additional resources for your readers that go Beyond the Book.

Some simple ways to go Beyond the Book include:

- Add an audio edition
- Add teaching videos
- Add a Facebook Group
- Add LIVE online sessions
- Add LIVE events
- Add 1-on-1 consultations

If we had met previous to your decision to write a book, I would have urged you not to write the book, <u>until</u> you have at least one of the above items ready to offer your readers.

The purpose of a book is not to make money.

The purpose is to change lives.

And the most powerful way to change other peoples' lives is by inviting them into a transformational relationship with you. So let me reframe another scary marketing term for you: lead magnet.

A lead magnet is a free gift you give away, in order to:

- Bless people
- Get people on your mailing list and into your circle of influence

Going Beyond the Book accomplishes at least two very important things for you as a Messenger: it increases both your impact and your income. Ask yourself if you want to do these two things:

1. Impact those looking for the help and hope you can provide.
2. Change your life by creating significant income doing what you were born to do.

The topic of Going Beyond The Book is beyond the scope of Successful Book Launch Secrets, but it's something I'll plan to cover in future volumes. But for now, as part of your new Marketing Mindset, I want you to at least realize: your book is just the beginning of what God wants to do through you.

In fact, as far as I'm concerned, the most amazing thing about becoming an author is *all the other doors and possibilities it will open for you.*

One very important step in building trust among potential book buyers is to create a strong AMAZON AUTHOR CENTRAL PAGE that establishes you as a messenger. You do that by:

- Including an appealing author photo.
- Adding a compelling bio.
- Uploading short videos.
- Integrating your blog feed, so that your posts are automatically added to Amazon.

You can check out my Amazon Author Page at AMAZON.COM/AUTHOR/DONNAPARTOW

I walk you step-by-step through creating your Amazon Author Page in my book, **_Getting Started on Amazon KDP_**.

STEP 2: CREATE YOUR SUPER HERO IDENTITY

WHO YOU ARE

It is vitally important for you to get crystal clear about who you are and who you help. This is absolutely essential when it comes time to launch your book and connect with potential book buyers.

One powerful way to do that is to **Create Your Super Hero Identity** following a two-step process:

> 1. Identify your anointed super-power
>
> 2. Name your Super Hero identity

Let's take a minute to look at each step. (I go into much greater depth on this at my annual LIFESTYLE FREEDOM EVENT: www.7daystofreedom.com

IDENTIFY YOUR ANOINTED SUPER-POWER

Take time to reflect deeply on who God created you to be. Consider your:

- Spiritual gifts

- Deepest core values
- Personality type
- Strengths
- Issues you are passionate about
- Life experiences
- What people COMPLIMENT you for
- How people are changed for the better because they met you

That last one is the most important. And really, it flows out of all of the other characteristics of who you are. Therefore, you should probably spend the most time pondering this question: "How are people changed for the better because they met me?"

It should be very close to what your book hopes to accomplish. As you were writing it, I'm sure you were asking yourself every step of the way, *"How will the reader's life be changed for the better because of reading my book?"*

If you did not take that approach, re-read your book with that question constantly at the forefront.

And, for sure, you need to constantly convey the answer throughout the Book Launch process. People will only buy your book if they are confident it will change their life for the better. It's your job to show them exactly how.

Okay, so now that you are clear about how their lives will be changed for the better, it's time to consider, "Why is YOUR book any different from the other books they might consider buying instead?" Why should the reader buy your book? What is it about you and the way you communicate that's going to be the difference-maker?

Ask God to reveal the very unique way you touch people's lives. What is it that sets you apart from every other author who is already addressing the same issues you feel called to write about?

Hint: There may be something about you that's non-conformist. You may be tempted to hide that aspect of who you are. Or try to compensate for it. But in the end, it may be <u>more effective</u> to simply embrace it.

When I began as a woman in ministry 40 years ago, every other female Christian communicator I read, saw or heard was a gentle, super-polite, happy homemaker who wore lace collars.

Guess what? My primary spiritual gifts are prophecy and discernment. Sad to say, the gifts of mercy and service are tied for dead-last. Plus I'm from New Jersey. Bundle all of that together and what do you get?

I see the truth – especially uncomfortable truths – and tend to blurt them out. If you tell me you have a problem, I'll see the deeper issue, confront you about it and tell you to get over yourself. Then I might even smack you upside the head.

Well okay, that was me in the early days of my walk with Jesus. Hopefully, I've gotten a tiny bit better over the years. Thank you, Holy Spirit.

I grew up with four older brothers and a truck-driving dad who was a World War II hero. All my favorite movies – and most of my sermon illustrations – are about sports and wars. When I was still speaking at women's conferences around the United States, I almost always wore military-themed suits and didn't even realize I was doing it.

Notice the woman holding work boots – those were my favorite prop: steel-tipped construction boots. I told the women they had to lace up their boots and get to work.

You can imagine how popular that made me on the Ladies Retreat circuit. Even in that photo, do I look like I'm fitting in?

I would end my events with clips from The Band of Brothers and tell ladies who had gathered for a **TEA PARTY** that they should forget about themselves and their own little families, slap a parachute on their backs and go behind enemy lines.

And I couldn't figure out why I didn't get any speaking referrals...

Eventually, I simply had to embrace my uniqueness. I'm a Jersey Girl who loves Jesus and a Kingdom Digital Nomad. I'll go anywhere in the world God sends me, parachute at the ready. I absolutely love going Behind Enemy Lines in some of the most dangerous places on earth.

My greatest gift is Mobilization or what I call my **"super-glue removal anointing."** God has given me a remarkable ability to convince people to get up and go, often to difficult or uncomfortable places. They end up scratching their heads, thinking, I can't believe she talked me into this...and having the time of their lives.

It's my anointed super power!

I've taken people with me to many

nations in Asia, Africa, Europe and Latin America.

If you're stuck and sick of being wrapped up in your own little world, I might be your new best friend. Just don't invite me to speak at your next ladies' luncheon. I'm the wrong person for that job.

And that's okay.

Is there something unique about you – that it's time for you to embrace? Could it be the very thing that will enable you to stand out in a crowd – and draw to yourself those who need what you carry?

What is your anointed super-power? That unique combination of traits God placed within you, which causes people to be changed because they encountered you.

That anointed super-power needs to be at the heart of every book you write – and everything you do during your Successful Book Launch process and beyond.

NAME YOUR SUPER HERO IDENTITY

The next step is to turn your "anointed super-power" into a Super Hero Identity. Yeah, I know, this might seem a little hokey. And it's okay if you never use it.

I haven't really used the word I came up with, either. But it helps me as I think about what I want to do in the world. And what should be my priority in terms of what I want to say and do during my Book Launch journey.

Me?

I'm **The Mobilizer**. Getting church people up out of the pews and into the world since 1980.

Right now, I'm asking God to enable me to use that super-power anointing in YOUR LIFE – to mobilize and motivate you to promote your book far and wide.

To mobilize is to "prepare and organize (troops) for active service." That's why I'm writing these words. Because I'm preparing YOU for active service.

Mobilize also means to "make movable or capable of movement." I hope this training program has made you capable of moving forward with your dream of becoming a widely-read author. I hope it inspires you to realize you are capable of turning the message of your book into a movement.

So far, I've resisted the temptation to publicly call myself **The Mobilizer**...but I might just do it someday. But in any case, my Super Hero Identity helps me remain clear about what I'm supposed to be doing with my time and energy.

ANSWER THESE TWO QUESTIONS

One exercise that many of my students have found helpful is exploring these two questions:

1. What do you stand for?
2. What do you stand against?

The answer to those two questions can bring tremendous clarity about why God has you on the planet in this hour. And why He is calling you to pro-actively market your book, taking a stand for _____ and a stand against _____. Go ahead and fill in those blanks.

Again, this will really shape your Book Launch strategy. If you didn't have this awareness during the first draft or first edition, go back and re-write any sections of the book that need more clarity.

Remind your readers frequently what it is you are calling them to.

Returning to my example, I stand for the church fully-mobilized, with every

Christian focused on the Great Commission. I stand against complacency and me-centered church-ianity.

Understanding what you stand for and what you stand against will be the difference between getting publicity for your Book Launch – or being ignored. No one wants to feature you on their blog or podcast just because you wrote a book. No one is going to write an article just to help you sell books.

But when you position yourself as someone launching a MOVEMENT – because there are things you stand for or things you stand against – all of a sudden, doors will open for you to proclaim your message. And in the process, successfully launch your book.

CREATE YOUR SUPER HERO AVATAR

Typically, in marketing, avatar refers to your ideal customer. And for sure, you should develop an avatar of your ideal reader (we'll talk about that next). But in this case, I'm suggesting you hire someone on fiverr.com to create an illustration of you in your Super Hero role. Again, even if you never use it publicly, it would make a great screen saver or wall poster.

I hired a woman in Ireland to draw this picture, based on a vision God gave me for my life. I am leading the way to uncharted territory, with the fire of God lighting the way, armed with the Word of God…plus a stylish purse and a tiara for good measure. (I probably should have had her paint a military-themed suit, but maybe I'm getting more feminine in my old age.)

This original watercolor was done for just $20 and it's a treasure. (Yes, I found her on fiverr!) Go to www.fiverr.com and search "original art work." Describe your Super Hero Identity and see what the artist comes up with!

This image is a daily reminder to me to follow the fire of the Holy Spirit and let that flame lead me forward, so that those who come behind me will go somewhere worth going. And the Word of God in my hand reminds me that the only book that lasts forever is His. He is perfect, I am not. My role is to proclaim His Word and walk in His ways, to the best of my strength. The rest is up to Him.

If you have your Super Hero Identity turned into a design, I'd love to see a copy of it. You can post it on any of the social media platforms and tag me. You can also come to my free Facebook Group called God's Soar Team

STEP 3: CLARIFY WHO YOU ARE TALKING TO

Once again, this is something that every author should be clear about before writing one word. And it will be absolutely critical as you being your Book Launch. Who are you talking to?

This one burning question will prevent you from making the grave mistake of writing for your own sake.

Writing for your own sake is called journaling.

Writing for catharsis is powerful…for you. But it typically has very little value for anyone else. UNLESS – and this is the wildcard that separates books that sell from books that don't –you constantly ask yourself, *"Who am I talking to…and what do I need to share that will make his/her life better?"* And *"How can I share my journey in a way that empowers the reader?"*

Again, this will be critical during the Book Launch. Before every post or podcast, before every Instagram Story or YouTube video, remind yourself of who you are talking to. Then share interesting information, inspiring stories and insightful truths – rather than simply saying, "Buy my book"

This is the key difference between a Book Launch that leaves you deflated and maybe even depressed – and one that changes your life forever. And I mean, changed for the better!

A video of you pleading with people to buy your new book is never going to go viral – *at least in a way that will help your cause.* But a video of you sharing compelling content definitely might.

Sometimes all that's needed is just a minor tweak. It means adding a sentence or two here or there, to bring it home for the reader or listener. How can they apply what you're talking about to their own lives, right now?

Notice how I have done that in the prior section as I described the process of finding your super-power anointing. I shared my story (because people relate to stories), but constantly brought it back to YOU and how you can apply my life experience to become clearer about who you are and the message you carry.

Why? So you can sell more books during your Book Launch and beyond.

Write/Speak to one person

If you write and speak as if you are talking to one person, then every person who reads your book or listens to you speaking will feel like you are talking directly to her or him.

That's the number one thing readers say to me, "I feel like you're talking to me! I feel like you know me! I feel like I know you!"

The simplest way to check your writing (and Book Launch promotional materials) to determine if it passes the test:

Do a global search for the words YOU, we and us. As in "we're in this together."

Avoid using "Christians," "parents," "wives," "some people," "everyone," and worst of all "one" as in "one cannot read too many books."

No one talks to a friend like that. And your book and Book Launch materials should talk to readers as if they are already friends. Because if you do, they will become incredibly loyal to you.

If you've already written your book…give it the "You" test. As you put together every aspect of your Book Launch, give everything the "You" test. **Make sure it's about the right YOU**. Not you, the author…but YOU, the reader/listener.

I encourage you to name your ideal reader. Write a vivid description of his or her life. What is her daily routine? What are his worries? What keeps her awake at night? What drives him to his knees in prayer in the morning?

When I began my writing career, my editor knew my test for every page of every book: *"I write for women in the bathroom."*

My ideal reader's name was Martha. She had an incredibly painful childhood and often felt trapped in her very difficult marriage. Martha wasn't raised in a Christian home but she woke up every day and tried her best to raise her children in a godly home.

Martha wanted to grow in her faith but she didn't have the time, space or mental bandwidth to sit at a desk with three translations of the Bible, Strong's Exhaustive Concordance, a workbook, a set of colored pens and a notebook.

In other words, Martha was never going

to sign up for a Kay Arthur Inductive Bible study. And if she did, she'd drop out feeling guilt-ridden and inadequate.

But she still wanted to grow in her faith. She still wanted to have daily time alone with God. But the only quiet place – the only time she could get any peace – was a few minutes in the bathroom.

That's why, if you've read any of my early books, you'll notice that each day's reading was super-short. Just a few pages. All Bible verses were **included on the page**. Martha was never told to "go look up such and such a passage" because I knew perfectly well – from personal experience – that her Bible wasn't in the bathroom. And Martha read my books while sitting on the toilet, hiding from her kids.

THAT is the kind of detail you need to know about your ideal reader. Can you describe him or her in that much depth? If not, before you attempt to launch your book, get absolute clarity about who your book is written for.

I promise you: this is the entire key to

writing and launching books that sell thousands, even tens of thousands or hundreds of thousands of copies. And remember, this isn't theory. I've lived it and proved it.

CREATE A READER AVATAR

Just as you created your Super Hero Identity avatar, now create one for your reader.

No, seriously. Do it!

Find a photo of your ideal reader. Print it out and post it near your writing space, so it's always in front of you. When you write, write as if you are penning a letter to <u>that one person</u>. It will change the way you write. I always wrote every word as if I was speaking directly to my friend, Martha.

It worked for me. It will work for you.

STEP 4: BUILD A LOYAL TRIBE OF PEOPLE

Now that you know who your ideal book buyer is, it's time to find lots more people just like him or her. It's time to Build a Loyal Tribe of People who will want to buy your book.

WHAT'S A TRIBE?

Well, entire books have been written on the subject. But in a nutshell, Tribe Members:

- Speak the same language (use the same lingo)
- Read the same books
- Listen to the same podcasts and audios
- Visit the same websites
- Follow the same thought leaders and influencers on Facebook, Instagram, YouTube, etc.
- Love the same ministers and worship leaders

Your ideal reader/book buyer is part of a larger Tribe. The great news is, **that Tribe is already gathering together**:

online and at conferences. Do you know where online and which conferences? You should — because that's the best place to share about your books!

FIND THE CURRENT TRIBE LEADERS

The first thing you should do is identify current Tribe Leaders. Many internet marketing experts recommend creating a Dream 100 List of the one hundred most influential people among those you feel called to reach.

The simplest way to do this is to think about who YOU follow. Or who YOU looked to when you were trying to find answers related to your book's topic.

Make a list of all your favorite:

- Authors
- Speakers
- Thought Leaders
- Ministries, Foundations and Non-profits
- Radio Shows

- TV Shows
- Podcasters
- Instagram Influencers
- YouTubers
- Facebook Influencers

List as many as you can possibly think of. Then to jog your memory and expand your list:

- Examine your bookshelf.
- Search through your Kindle book collection.
- Pick your favorite Podcaster – and make a list of all of their guests. Add them to your list.
- Find out if your favorite leaders host a live event. Add anyone they have invited to speak on their platform to your list.
- Repeat the process with all of the other platforms.

It shouldn't take you more than a few hours to develop this list and it's one of the most important things you can ever do to maximize exposure for your book.

Your mission is to connect with your Dream 100. Begin by praying and asking God for favor. Then find out how you can honor and bless THEM, long before you ever ask them to do something for you.

Sow where you want to go.

Think: What do you want these 100 people to do for you? Is there any way you can do it for *them*? You certainly want them to say great things about your book! So there's a place to start.

Go write terrific reviews for each of their books, podcast episodes, YouTube videos, etc.

Never ask someone to do for you something that you have not first done for others.

Jesus said it even better in The Golden Rule: "Do unto others as you would have them do unto you."

By the way, when a person of influence goes out of their way to help you, **be grateful and show it**. No one owes you their endorsement.

One of the greatest regrets of my 40

years in ministry is that I was not nearly grateful enough to those people who endorsed my work and opened doors of opportunity to me. Please don't make that mistake.

G iven that there is already an army of well-established experts out there, it's easy to wonder: "Why should anyone listen to me? They are already listening to so and so...and I can never be as amazing and influential as so and so!"

Let me tell you a little secret.

MOST people would be very happy if someone – just a few steps ahead of them—was willing to lend them a hand. Let's face it: some mega-superstar with a million books in print or a million Instagram followers simply doesn't have the time to give personal attention to everyone who is following them.

That's where **you** come in! You can reach out to some of those millions of followers and let them know, *"I can help you implement what you are learning from the pros. I'll walk with you every step of the way."*

An Influencer can **be someone who is on the same journey** as the rest of the Tribe.

Did you catch that? Okay, let me say it again. It's that important.

An Influencer can <u>be someone who is on the same journey</u> as the rest of the Tribe.

The entire key is to constantly stay just one step ahead. Not miles ahead. Just a step. So you can reach back and share what you've learned and how you are applying it to your own life. That's what's known as a Leading Learner. And it's very powerful. In fact, many Mega-Influencers began as Leading Learners.

I just read a book by a guy who is making a 6-figure income helping people write books. He launched his business after helping exactly one person write one book.

That may not sound like much. But it's more than most people have ever done. He's making a great income as a Leading Learner.

HOW DO YOU BECOME A LEADING LEARNER?

It's not complicated. And I'm 100% confident you can do it. Wake up each day an hour earlier than you currently do. I don't care if you wake up at 5am. Ask God for strength to wake up at 4am.

Study for that one hour.

Then share what you just learned in a Facebook Post, Instagram Story or short video. Condense that 1-hour into just a few minutes. That's a valuable public service for your fellow Tribe members – you know, the ones who need that same information but didn't wake up an hour early to study.

Do this for one full year and report back to me how it worked out. There's literally no way that level of diligence cannot pay off.

Give. Give. Give. Deposit. Deposit. Deposit.

When you are leading the way – even if you're only one step ahead – those following you will naturally want to buy your book and tell their friends about it. All of those deposits will be in your account when it's time to make a withdrawal in the form of asking people to buy and recommend your book.

LEARN THE LANGUAGE

How on earth can you be heard above the noise? In fact, there's an entire book on the subject called, **Platform: Get Heard Above the Noise** by Michael Hyatt. He's always the smartest guy in any room, so you might want to check it out.

Meanwhile, here's my take on how to be heard.

I've traveled in ministry to more than 40 nations on six continents. *(Let me know if you want to come with me on a cruise to Antarctica because, for sure, I have to do that before I die. Just so I can say I've been to all seven continents! But I digress…)*

Few things are more overwhelming than being in a crowd of people, all of them speaking a language I don't understand. There have been moments when I truly thought my brain would explode.

Then comes that glorious moment when, in the midst of all that noise, I hear someone speaking my language. Waves of relief flood over me and I run to that person and cling to them with all I've got. I don't care if that person is an English professor. I just care that they can speak the same language and we can understand each other.

We are drawn to people who speak the same language we do. And people will be drawn to you when you learn to speak their language. (It will also help to use the correct keywords, but that's for another book, **Getting Started on Amazon KDP**!).

One of the quickest ways to learn the language of your tribe is by using the First Look feature on Amazon. This is the coolest hack ever:

1. Find the 10 best-selling books that your Tribe members have read or are reading.
2. Turn to the Table of Contents
3. Write out all the keywords listed in the chapter titles.
4. Most books have at least 10 chapters.
5. Write out every word that isn't "a," "and," or "the" etc.
6. You should have at least 200 words. Probably more.
7. Analyze which of these words might be unique to your Tribe.

You've just discovered the language of your Tribe. Just as a small example, Presbyterians wouldn't use the chapter title "Moving in the Prophetic" but someone in the Prophetic Movement certainly would. Presbyterians will talk about John Calvin and the total depravity of man. There's two topics you could sit in a charismatic church for 100 years and never hear mentioned! Be alert to buzz words and phrases that call out to potential readers, *"We speak the same language."*

Keyword research is beyond the scope of this book. However, if you can wrap your brain around keywords, then write blog posts, record videos and create social media posts using #hashtags that feature the most popular keywords, you will sell far more books than you otherwise would.

NAME YOUR TRIBE

N ow go the extra step and think of a name for your Tribe. This is surprisingly powerful and authors who go this extra step will lift up a voice that's heard above the noise.

My original Tribe was known as PWAs – Princesses with Attitude. We had mugs and t-shirts that sold like crazy at my events. Everyone wanted to identify as part of the Tribe. Women would show up wearing tiaras and waving light-up princess wands. It was great fun.

It caught on like wildfire in churches and next thing you know, being a Princess was all the rage in every church pew. My mass movement had begun!!! Woo hoo!!!

Then, of course, the idea was co-opted by someone who heard me give the message and hired a ghostwriter who turned it into a New York Times bestselling book.

And that might just happen to you someday. It's okay. God will give you a fresh idea to run with. And as my mother always said, "Imitation is the sincerest form of flattery."

That's part of launching a movement – it takes on a life of its own. And that is what you want to do, rather than just launching a book. **You want to launch a movement.** Far more powerful. And ultimately, you might just have an army of imitators. How flattering!

It was similar to what happened with Rick Warren's book, **The Purpose-Driven Life**. It took off like crazy. Next thing you know, hundreds of other authors, speakers, and organizations picked up the mantle and ran with it. It wasn't just a book anymore. It was a movement.

BUILD YOUR LIST AND SOCIAL MEDIA FOLLOWING

I f you ever decide to pursue traditional publishing, the first question a potential agent or publisher will ask is, "Tell me about your platform."

Your platform is code for "How many people are already in your Tribe?"

Why do they want to know that? Because they are already thinking ahead to your Book Launch – and you should be thinking ahead, too.

The quickest way to build your platform is to find out where your potential Tribe members are already gathering, so you can connect with them and get your message in front of them. Here are some ways to do just that:

GOOGLE

Type your topic + forum into the Google search bar. You'll find hundreds if not thousands of online forums where people are already gathered to discuss the issue. Join the 10 most popular forums.

FACEBOOK

Go to the Facebook search bar and type in your topic + group. Of the thousands of Groups already formed, identify 20 to join and begin participating. Look for Facebook Groups with more than 20,000 members.

BLOGS

Search your topic + blog. Or simply search in Google for urls that might be a blog format and check them out. Find the 10 most popular blogs in your niche that have guest bloggers. Offer to do blog swaps if your blog is active enough; otherwise, write amazingly well, be consistently engaged and persistent in connecting.

There are many companies who will arrange blog tours for authors and some who focus specifically on Christian authors. If you have a marketing budget, that might be worth exploring.

PODCASTS

Search on iTunes. Identify the 10 most popular podcasts among your Tribe members that feature guests. Make it your goal to become a guest someday.

You can hire companies who will market you to podcasters.

You might consider launching your own podcast. Then, rather than asking to be invited, you can do the inviting. As a result, you may get a return invite. That's the smart way to do it.

And of course, the time to do the inviting is long before your Book Launch. So the time for return events will be…during your Book Launch!

FORM JOINT VENTURE (JV) PARTNERSHIPS

You have already identified 100 of the most influential people who are currently speaking to your tribe. Those with large social media followings and substantial mailing lists. Once you've developed a paid program (Minimum price point of $197 and significantly higher would be better), you can invite these influencers to promote a package that includes your book and paid program in return for a 50% commission.

People used to be willing to promote lower-cost items ($97). But the market is flooded. Today, most Influencers will not share with their list unless they stand to earn $1,000 or more per sale.

If you do decide to develop paid programs that you offer in partnership with Joint Ventures, check out Samcart. It's one of the best online services in my arsenal – and I've worked with dozens of companies during the past twenty-plus years online.

DO IT LONG BEFORE THE BOOK LAUNCH

To truly be effective, all of this foundational work needs to be done months, and even years in advance. For example, the time to become active in all those Facebook Groups and forums isn't the day you release your book. That is tacky tacky tacky!

If this strategy is going to work, you'll need to truly BELONG to these various networks and develop real relationships with key influencers – not just bug them because you are trying to sell your book. That will never work.

In other words, realistically, you might not have it done in time for your first book. The purpose of your first book is often just to **position you as an Authority**. Then, from that position as a #1 best-selling Amazon author (I teach you exactly how to do that in **Getting Started on Amazon KDP**), you can then use the above strategies to:

1. Keep your book selling for years and years.

2. CRUSH the Book Launch for your second book by connecting with those influencers from a position of credibility.

How exciting is that?

STEP 5: CAPTURE ATTENTION WITH YOUR BOOK DESCRIPTION

After all of that time and effort, guess what? You have a grand total of about three seconds to grab someone's attention on Amazon. It helps to have a terrific book cover that is appealing even when it's reduced to the size of a thumbnail – which is the only way most potential readers will ever see your book.

But right after the title, sub-title and cover, the most important thing that will sell books is a terrific Amazon Book Description.

EMPHASIZE THE BENEFITS

Think of your Book Description as a sales page, rather than a book report. Your purpose isn't to write a summary so they know what it's about. It's to convince people that your book can solve their problems.

How will your book make their life better? Why do they need to read it right now? What makes it unique and uniquely effective?

In order to do that, you need to write scannable text – with bullet points, **bold**

letters and *italics* – not long paragraphs.

THE HOOK

Write a brief "hook" to grab attention. You can do that with any of the following strategies:

- Shocking Statistic
- Surprising Fact
- Controversial Claim
- Bold Promise
- Thought-Provoking Question

This only needs to be a sentence; two at the most.

The ideal way to create your hook is to finish the statement: "What if I told you..." then fill in the rest of it with any item from the bullet list (a bold promise, controversial claim, etc). (I'm indebted to Rob Eagar for this concept. His books on marketing for authors are among the best I've read.)

Next, write a super-short paragraph (three sentences max) that outlines the issues your book addresses, then list 5 bullet points summarizing 5 specific ways the book will help the reader.

These should, ideally, be 5 things they'll be able to **do** differently.

Too often, Christian authors talk about how their books will help people believe differently – but people can listen to thousands of free sermons online that will help them believe differently.

They buy books because they want to **DO** something differently. Make sure your bullet points are specific and benefit oriented. A good bullet point always includes the answer to the burning question in every potential reader's mind: "So what?"

Example: Learn 3 simple ways to memorize scripture so you can easily recall a passage even years later.

Why do they need to buy your book? To learn three simple scripture memory techniques. So what? So they can recall passages years after they first memorize them.

Include another paragraph or two summarizing what sets your book apart and how the reader's life will be better if they buy it.

5 WORDS TO USE

Try to weave all five of these words into your description at least once. You can use the word YOU an unlimited number of times.

1. You
2. Free
3. Instantly
4. Because
5. New

If you've done thorough keyword research, be sure to include the exact keywords you listed within Amazon KDP (See **Getting Started on Amazon KDP**) somewhere within your Book Description.

Also, be sure to mention that there's an offer within the book for a free (there's that word) _____ - whatever you are offering as your lead magnet, whether it's an audio version of the book, a companion video training program, online class, Facebook Support Group, etc.

Then you add, "Because..." and tell them why you want to bless them with that free gift. There, I've almost written your Book Description for you! You're welcome.

By the way, the best possible thing to offer the reader is a free audio version of the same book. I've not done that yet, but it's high on my list of things to get done. It's my understanding, from talking with other authors, that up to 70% of readers will opt-in (i.e. join your mailing list) when you make them that offer.

PROVIDE A CALL TO ACTION

Finally, include a call to action. Urge the prospective reader to **Get the Book Today** or **Scroll Up to Order Now**.

It may seem obvious, but most Book Descriptions fail to issue a Call to Action. And it does make a difference.

Check out The Book Description Generator created by Dave Chesson and currently available free on Kindlepreneur.com. Be aware that, at some point, he may charge for access to it and honestly, he should. It's an amazing tool and should require payment to access.

He also offers free templates on how to craft a great Book Description. His website is absolutely outstanding and I'm amazed how many resources he offers at no charge.

There are a wide variety of people offering the service of writing book descriptions on fiverr.com. So far, I haven't found one that I can recommend. But new people join all the time, so it might be worth checking it out.

STEP 6: SHOW SOCIAL PROOF TO POTENTIAL BUYERS

People are fearful of making a wrong decision.

Hearing from others who made the same decision with great results is very reassuring. That's what social proof is all about. And that's why reviews are super-important to your Book Launch.

Be very aggressive in obtaining positive reviews. And make it easy for people who already love you to review your book. Your goal should be to have 10 reviews on the first day. This is accomplished by providing key people with an ARC – **Advanced Reading Copy**. Then, the day the book is released, they purchase a copy on Amazon and can immediately provide an honest review.

You should get an ARC into the hands of your most ardent fans at least two weeks before you release the book. GIVE THEM A DEADLINE to write an honest review. Have them post in a Facebook Group or email it to you. Just for accountability's sake.

Then, the minute your book is officially

released, ask them to post their already-prepared review on Amazon. They must buy a copy first so they can write a Verified Review. Otherwise, they will need to add a disclaimer that they received the book for free in return for a review. (More details in a minute.)

Now here's the problem.

Left to themselves, people won't bother to write book reviews. Unless of course, they are a deranged hater. Then they will move hell and earth to track you down on Amazon where they'll write an essay, ripping apart every aspect of your book. Not content with that, they'll email you (expecting a personal reply) and comment on every social media platform to let the world know what a terrible, no good, horrible author you are.

But the people who love you?

Not so much. Unless you make it easy for them to show the love. Fortunately, I've got another hack up my sleeve for you. Once you have set up your book in Amazon KDP, find your ASIN or ISBN-10 number. Then add it to the end of this

URL:

HTTP://AMAZON.COM/REVIEW/CREATE-REVIEW?&ASIN=

Previously, when you asked people to "go write a review on Amazon," it involved a bit of effort on their part. They had to find your book page, scroll down to the bottom and hunt around for where it says, "Write a Review." Then click a few more buttons.

Most people are busy.

They don't want to put in that much effort toward an optional activity in the midst of a zillion obligations. Now, thanks to this super-cool url, you can send them a link that will take them directly to the screen where they just type in the review. It will look something like the screenshot on the following page.

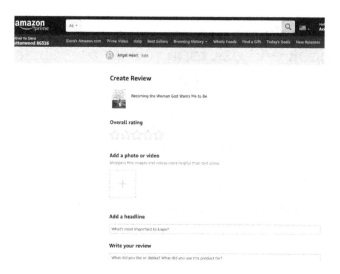

So, for example if you love my book, **Becoming the Woman God Wants Me To Be**, you can just go here to write a review to lift up your very favorite Jersey Girl author:

HTTP://AMAZON.COM/REVIEW/CREATE-REVIEW?&ASIN=0800728351

Since paperback readers can't click hyperlink, I created what's called a Pretty link to make it easy to find:

https://donnapartow.com/review-launch

Go ahead. I'll wait for you to come back…

You wrote the review, right? Right?

Hmmm…….see what I mean?

Final tip: Add this direct url to the end of your book and ask for a review as people turn the last page and your book is fresh on their minds. If you don't know the url when you upload the first edition, no worries at all.

If you book is self published, you can easily upload a revised copy of your manuscript as many times as you like. Amazon doesn't mind.

And this markting advantage, for sure, is worth uploading a revised edition.

If it's traditionally published, provide this information to your publisher and be sure they add it the future editions.

EDITORIAL REVIEWS

You can add Editorial Reviews on your book description page within KDP or you can log-in to Amazon Author Central, click the Book Tab and you'll have many more options to add content, including a message from your heart to the potential reader and any Editorial Reviews.

(Again, I cover the technical aspects in my book, **Getting Started on Amazon KDP**.)

When I say Editorial, I mean famous people! Be sure to seek out key influencers and proactively pursue win-win relationships with them.

So yes, you should and <u>MUST</u> send free copies to Influencers. That's who your ARCs are really intended for: people with a massive following who can make all the difference in your Book Launch. (Remember your Dream 100 list?)

If you manage to secure reviews from magazines or trade journals, be sure to add those as well.

WHAT NOT TO DO

Here are some things you should never do:

- Do NOT pay for reviews (as offered on fiverr.com and elsewhere on the internet).

- You **cannot** request 5-star or positive reviews. This is a violation of Amazon's Terms of Service. You are only permitted to ask for "an honest review."

And that's what you always want: honest reviews. Please, we are Christians. Don't try to "game the system." Amazon is infinitely smarter than we might be tempted to believe.

- **Update on a gray area:** Amazon will currently allow you to ask family members to review your book. However, they must disclose their relationship to you. Amazon knows an amazing amount of information about their users and if a relative posts a review without disclosing the relationship, it will be deleted.

So it's definitely not okay for your mom to write a supposedly objective glowing review. But Amazon may (or may not) let it stand if she writes, "This is my son's book and I couldn't be prouder." Then explains how she has seen you implement your teachings.

Don't be surprised if reviews written by your friends disappear soon after they are posted. If Amazon determines that you have a pre-existing connection (let's say, you shipped them a book or even flowers sometime in the past), they will remove it.

- **You are <u>not allowed</u> to give away free copies in return for a review UNLESS it is disclosed.** In my view, the Amazon Disclaimer Policy eliminates the effectiveness of giving away free copies to amateur book reviewers.

There's actually a small army of these bookaholics who live for – *and will solicit from you* – free books "in return for a review." This game was more popular before Amazon said, "That's fine, but you are <u>required</u> to add 'I received a free copy of this book to review.'"

If some random person asks me for a "review copy" of my book, the answer is always a quick and decisive, "No way Jose!" You can get it on Kindle for less than five bucks. That's not a latte.

I've also observed that some of these bookaholics-seeking-freebies tend to be hyper-critical. They may even try to inflate their own sense of self-importance by nitpicking your book to death.

Can you tell I don't think giving away free copies of your book to amateur book critics is a smart move?

As of this writing, Amazon does not require reviewers to purchase the book to write a review. However, they may soon require that all reviews are by Verified Purchasers only.

Honestly, I think they should. Currently, anyone who has spent more than $50 on Amazon within the past year can write a review of any book. Even if they've never read it. I don't think that's fair. But Amazon didn't ask my opinion.

Amazon mitigates against the obvious abuse this invites by giving more weight in their algorithm to a Verified Purchase. They even include a moniker for the benefit of potential book buyers, as well. But not everyone has the good sense to factor Verified Purchase into their book-buying equation. This is one thing I hope Amazon will change in the near future.

AMAZON POLICY

R ead and memorize this policy. If you are caught violating it, your book will be permanently removed and you may be banned from the platform:

"We consider incentives to be any type of reward that is given in return for a Customer Review, including but not limited to bonus content, entry to a contest or sweepstakes, discounts on future purchases, and other gifts."

I am amazed to see people actively violating this rule. Very foolish and short-sighted, in my view.

IMPORTANT CLARIFICATION

Y ou ARE permitted to provide all those same incentives for people to **purchase your book.** In fact, the secret to a mega-Book Launch is to create an irresistible package of bonus materials, prizes, giveaways, etc. And make it available to everyone who can prove they bought your book.

That's perfectly okay. In fact, it's better

than okay. It's Brilliant Book Launch Marketing. If you are savvy enough to pull it off, go for it.

I sold more than 3,000 copies of **Becoming the Woman God Wants Me To Be** in a matter of days when I offered to do a FREE Live class on Facebook. The price of admission was the purchase of the book. Of course, that was back before anyone else had ever done such a thing, so it was truly a sensation. (This is how far "back in the day" it was. I had to email the ladies an instructional video explaining what Facebook was plus step-by-step guidance on how to join...I kid you not.)

Now, of course, it's a commonplace strategy. As a result, it's likely to be somewhat less effective.

But still, you could certainly count on selling dozens if not hundreds of copies of your book with a simple offer like that. With a large enough email list, you could sell thousands. In fact, this is a pillar in the strategy to make the New York Times bestseller list.

Buy the book. Get the class for free. Works incredibly well.

Eventually, I decided it was far more lucrative to sell the CLASS and give away the book for free. But then those people – my biggest fans! – were not permitted to review the book on Amazon. Why? Because I made the mistake of shipping directly from Amazon to the students, so all of them were instantly and permanently connected to me.

Bummer. Major bummer.

Well, as they say, it's always something.

SUPER COOL TIP I PLAN TO IMPLEMENT

Rather than shipping people the book (as I did) or requiring a receipt to "prove" they really purchased your book (like most authors do during their Book Launch), here's a better idea.

Make the price of admission to the free class a PHOTO of the prospective student holding up their **paperback copy** of the book. Once they **tag you** in the photo on Facebook, they are admitted to the Facebook Group where the course materials will be provided.

Be sure to let book buyers know, it's not enough to post a picture of the book. It has to be <u>their face</u> holding up the book.

This is pure genius. I don't remember who I first saw doing it, but I gotta say, I wish I had thought of that one myself.

That's what we call next-level **Book.Launch.Genius.**

WHAT TO DO TO CREATE SOCIAL PROOF

Okay, so now that we've covered the basics of what Social Proof is and you've heard a bunch of stern warnings about What Not To Do, let's move to the fun topic of What To Do.

Inquiring minds want to know: Donna, how do you REALLY sell hundreds of thousands of books? Here it is:

1. Write great books.

2. Build a massive community of people who need your books – and who are loyal to you because you've first invested in them. These are the "raving fans" who can't wait to buy your book the minute it's released.

3. Promote your books far and wide while providing enough goodwill that people want to write reviews to create Social Proof.

4. Learn to ask for help. It takes a village to sell lots of books. You

can't do it alone. And people are too busy to guess what you need. Make specific "asks" of people and give them specific instructions with clear deadlines, so they know exactly how to do the most good. People are more inclined to cooperate when there is a deadline involved.

5. Of course, make plenty of deposits before you attempt a withdrawal – that applies to all relationships – see #2.

That's it? Yep, that's it.

But that's a lot of "it." All of the foundational work for your marketing campaign needs to be done months, even years, in advance. That's why, as you'll recall, the first question a traditional publisher asks is *"How's your platform?"*

What they mean is: *"How many DEPOSITS have you already made?"* Because they know that a Successful Book Launch will require plenty of demands on those deposits. And now you know that, too.

Please don't hit "publish" then think about generating a ton of Social Proof. You'd be amazed how often people do that very thing.

BECOME ACTIVE ON GOODREADS

D id you know there's an entire social media platform devoted to books? Did you know that millions of book lovers gather online to talk about books, review books, recommend books and generally celebrate the written word?

It's called Goodreads and you should definitely make it a priority as you seek to build Social Proof.

Think about this:

No one goes on Facebook for the sole purpose of talking about books. They go on Facebook to share pictures of their families and to see what their friends are up to. Yes, they may belong to some Facebook Groups related to their favorite author, but that's not their sole purpose for being on the platform. They are there to socialize.

No one goes on Twitter for the sole purpose of talking about books. They go to comment on the current news cycle, to debate about politics or to watch the latest public feud.

Yes, there are some Twitterati devoted to sharing books – especially free or 99 cent books. But it's not the primary reason people are on Twitter.

The same is true of Instagram, TikTok, YouTube and the rest of the social media platforms.

If you are looking for book lovers, the place to be is Goodreads, which currently has 90 million members. As always, be sure you begin making plenty of deposits long before your Book Launch. Don't expect to show up and simply promote your book. That won't work.

Be an involved member of the community. Having said that, full-disclaimer: I'm not active in commenting. However, I am an avid Kindle book reader and a highlighting-fanatic. Whenever I finish reading a book, I share all of my highlights on Goodreads. That's one simple way to make a worthwhile deposit.

Also, be sure to link your Amazon account to Goodreads. Then, whenever you post a review on Amazon, it is automatically shared on Goodreads. Remember to "do unto others" by writing book reviews of every good book you read.

Each of those reviews is a powerful deposit.

The fastest way to get started on Goodreads is to integrate it with your Amazon account. Goodreads will then automatically add all books you purchase on Kindle to Goodreads. You can also set it up to share all of your Amazon book reviews automatically on Goodreads. So you are making double deposits! You can organize your books into Shelves by topic.

Next, integrate Goodreads with your Facebook and Twitter account. Goodreads will then search for and add your friends from those platforms to your Goodreads connections. As you add new friends on those platforms, remember to return to Goodreads and do a new search. It's fast and easy. (Perhaps mark your calendar to do this once per month.)

There's a good book you can read that covers the basics of how to get started on Goodreads. It's called **An Author's Guide to Goodreads** by Barb Drozdowich.

Social Proof on a social platform filled with book lovers? That's about as powerful as it gets! Be sure to include Goodreads in your overall book marketing strategy.

The time to become an active, contributing member of Goodreads is now...not when your book is released.

GETTING STARTED ON GOODREADS

1. Become a Member.

2. Add books to your Virtual Shelves.

3. Claim your book.

4. Convert your profile to an Author Profile.

5. Add the RSS Feed from your Blog.

6. Upload videos and photos.

7. Schedule a Goodreads Giveaway.

Active Goodreads members who enter the giveaway will likely add your book to their "Want to Read" shelf. When they do, it jumps into the newsfeed. If you have hundreds of people entering the giveaway contest, it will automatically create a lot of buzz, with your book popping up over and over again in newsfeeds.

8. Add Lists with Listopia.

   Listopia is a great way to position your book alongside relevant best-sellers. Don't add your book to 20 lists in one day. And definitely don't add it to irrelevant lists. Far better to add your book to one per week. A deep dive on Listopia is beyond the scope of this book, but if you join and enjoy Goodreads, it's definitely worth exploring.

9. Add the Goodreads Widget to your Website.

STEP 7: BUILD MOMENTUM WITH PROMOTIONS

SET YOUR LAUNCH DATE

N ow you are finally ready to launch your book. The first step is to **Set Your Launch Date** or find out the date that has been set for you by your publisher.

Plan at least a month ahead of time to start spreading the word that the book is on the way. Pick a Wednesday. Then, if you are self-published, you will run a free promotion for 3 days (Wednesday, Thursday and Friday) building momentum for your book as you head into the weekend.

That's important, because most people buy Kindle books on Saturdays.

(If you are traditionally published, your publisher may still agree to do a special offer on the ebook edition. I have offered several of my books for just $1.99 with my publisher's cooperation.)

If Amazon sees lots of momentum behind your book heading into the weekend, they may even promote it for you.

Once upon a time, it was a sure-thing that

your momentum on the Free List would automatically land you in great position when your book switches over to the Paid List. It's no longer guaranteed, since Amazon has changed their algorithm. But you still have a great chance of getting picked up on their **Hot New Releases**.

And that's right where you want to be when everyone wakes up on Saturday morning, looking for a good book to read during their day off.

MAKING THE LIST

I'm not sure anyone else will come out and admit this, but the Jersey Girl is about to serve it up straight for you: It's a bit of a game. And the name of the game is to give your book the cachet of **"#1 Amazon Best Seller."** The surest way to do that is to…give your book away for free.

I know, I know. If it's free, how is it a best **seller**? If you want to be absolutely precise in your language, just say **#1 on Amazon**. That still sounds very credible, right?

Here's how it works. Amazon actually has two lists for each category of Kindle Books – and both are listed under the header of Amazon Best Sellers. Look at the two screenshots on the following page and see if you can see the difference. (Seriously, go look!)

At first glance, you probably can't.

But if you look very carefully at both screenshots, you'll notice that in the first one (featuring **Becoming the Woman God Wants Me To Be** in the #1 position) there is an orange line under Top 100 Paid. And in the second screenshot, featuring the book **God Confidence** in the #1 position, there is an orange line under Top 100 Free.

If you didn't notice the orange line – and you almost certainly didn't until I brought it to your attention – no one in your circle of influence will either.

All they will see is the screenshot featuring YOUR BOOK in the #1 position under a giant banner that says Amazon Best Sellers.

And that's all you need at this phase of your writing journey: instant credibility thanks to the Amazon Seal of Approval.

Within a week or two, doors will begin to open. I've just heard from two students I've helped who both received speaking invitations as a direct result of posting screenshots like this on their social media accounts.

Actually, one of the most important things to do during your Kindle Free Promotion Days is to take lots of screenshots and share them with the world.

There's no better way to generate lots of enthusiasm for your brand-new book! Your family, friends and future Tribe members will all be incredibly impressed by all of this.

Instantly, you'll become the Authority! You're not only an author – you made it to #1 on Amazon.

In general, the purpose of your book is to:

1. Establish you as an authority

2. Build a mailing list to grow your Tribe

Notice that "make lots of money selling books" is not listed. Because very few people – not even one in a million—can make money just by selling books. But THOUSANDS upon thousands of authors have used a book to solidify their position as an expert, enabling them to attract a large following and increase their prices on speaking gigs, coaching, consulting, online classes, etc.

There are some other things that a self-published book cannot accomplish. That's why I've chosen to be a hybrid author, doing a combination of traditionally-published and self-published books. But given that it is nearly impossible for an unknown author to get a book deal, if you do it right, self-publishing for the express purpose of establishing yourself as an authority might be the best way to land a traditional book deal in the future.

Just keep in mind, you will have to write a new book if and when the traditional publishing door opens. Almost no publisher will take on a previously self-published book; but many will clamor for the chance to work with you on future book projects if you handle your self-published Book Launch correctly

ESTABLISH YOURSELF AS AN AUTHORITY

If your only goal – *and it's a worthy one to be sure*—is to establish yourself as an authority, then it may be worth doing the FREE book giveaway just to accomplish that.

And if you follow my instructions in **Getting Started on Amazon KDP** so you can select the right keywords and categories, you are almost guaranteed Top 10 in your category. In fact, you are very likely – almost guaranteed—to hit #1.

BUILD YOUR MAILING LIST TO GROW YOUR TRIBE

P lease do not launch your book – and for sure, do not attempt Step 7 – until you have a simple Lead Magnet ready to get people on your list. Otherwise, you will have absolutely no idea who downloaded your book and you'll have no way of getting in touch with them. That really defeats one of the top reasons for giving away free ebooks. Namely, building your list.

The easiest and most obvious lead magnets are either:

1. An audio version of the book

2. A video teaching related to the book

Please consider creating one of those two offers before your Book Launch. I promise, you will be very glad you did.

Ideally, you should also have a paid product available to offer. You can learn more about this vital process in my online training class, Take Your Message to the World, which you can learn more about at www.donnapartow.com/message. But even if you don't have that available, as long as you have a good lead magnet, you can move forward.

By the way, some great things to offer include:

- Online Class Based on the Book
- Private Consultations
- 1-on-1 Coaching
- Group Coaching
- Monthly Membership Club
- Virtual Summit
- Live Event

I train people how to create programs like that at my annual Lifestyle Freedom Event. Go to www.7daystofreedcom.com to find out about our upcoming destination. It's always held in spectacular locations like Fiji, Costa Rica...even an Irish castle!

WHEN TO OFFER YOUR

Your KDP Select Promotional period doesn't have to be the first day your book is released. In fact, it shouldn't be. There will inevitably be glitches and errors you catch. So don't share it with the whole wide world – just your close circle of influence.

These free days do not need to be consecutive either. In fact, I strongly recommend dividing them into one 3-day promotion (early in the 90 days; ideally 5-7 days after you hit publish). Then another 2-day promotion around 10-14 days later.

IMPORTANT: You only have the first 30 days to make it onto Amazon's Hot New Releases. The clock starts the minute you hit "publish to Kindle." That's one super-important reason why you should have three of your smartest friends search the book for errors before you upload it to KDP. And why you should download the free Kindle Previewer Software from Amazon. The Previewer is intended to show you exactly how your book will look on a variety of electronic devices.

Be sure to take these all-important extra steps before you hit publish. I know you are excited. Trust me, I get it. I've made this mistake myself. I was so happy to have the book done, that I just wanted to share it with the world.

Wrong move. There were glitches galore!

It shouldn't take more than a week to get feedback from your friends (give them a deadline). And it shouldn't take more than 48-72 hours to fix any glitches you find in the Kindle Previewer. It's worth the wait.

DESIGN SOCIAL MEDIA IMAGES

Either hire someone on Fiverr.com or use Canva to create images and banners promoting your book release. You will be sharing this via email and on all of your social media platforms.

Here's an example:

"FREE KINDLE" BLOGS AND GROUPS

There are literally thousands of blogs, forums and Facebook Groups that promote free ebooks. An increasing number of them charge you a fee to promote your free book. At this point, stick with the sites that do not charge a fee. That's because the most influential promotion sites (BookBub and

BuckBooks) will require your book to have a track record with at least 10 reviews before they even consider taking your money from you.

Most of these promotion sites require at least 7 days advance notice and longer is preferable. I had originally included a list of these promotion sites in this book, but it's now clear to me that most of these sites come and go pretty quickly.

So rather than including a list that will probably be outdated the day I hit publish on this book, here's a link to the Kindlepreneur website page featuring the top Kindle Promotion Sites. Dave Chesson, who runs the site, is on top of things and is your best source for updates on the best free (and paid) promotion sites.

TIMING MATTERS

Have everyone in your circle of influence go download the book **at the same time**.

This makes a huge difference because Amazon ranks are updated hourly.

Be sure to leverage your email list and social media following. You can even run a "Don't Download My Book YET" Campaign. And make it a fun thing. Do a LIVE Broadcast with a countdown to when you want everyone to go download it.

My ebooks instantly make it to the Amazon best-seller list with a single email because I've built my list to nearly 50,000 subscribers. Build your list!

Meanwhile, do all you can on social media to build excitement around the Free Book Promotion.

Monitor your book hourly for sales rank. Your goal is the Top 100 in the Kindle Free Store. You <u>CAN</u> achieve this goal if you handle your Book Launch correctly.

STEP 8: CONSIDER PAID PROMOTIONS TO CONTINUE MOMENTUM

Recall in the prior section that I recommended using only 3 of your 5 Free Kindle Promotion Days. What do you do with the other two days?

Consider Investing in Paid Book Promotion to Continue Momentum! This should be done once you have gotten at least twenty-five 5-star reviews.

You can use your additional two days at any time before the 90 days is up. I suggest using them as soon as you hit the targeted number of reviews or around Day 45, whichever comes first.

You can find a list of the most popular book promotion sites on Kindlepreneur.com. There's also a good recap of the top promotion sites with videos showing actual campaign results at PaidAuthor.com As mentioned, there's a lot of turnover, so I'm only going to mention the giants in the industry.

There are still free book promotion sites, including thousands of Facebook Groups devoted to sharing free books. You should join them far in advance of your book's official release date. Just type

Free Books in the Facebook Search bar.

BUCKBOOKS

BUCKBOOKS has a massive email list of book lovers. Each day, they email deals on books priced at 99 cents or below. They cover every genre, from non-fiction to fiction. They specialize in new releases and the cost for a paid promotion is currently around $29.

THEIR STATED GUIDELINES ARE:

- Write a great book.
- Have positive reviews.
- Book length: 10,000 words or more.
- Appeal to a broad audience.
- Professionally-designed cover.

EREADER NEWS TODAY

EREADER NEWS TODAY sends a daily email of book deals, customized to each of their half-million subscribers. To be considered, your book must meet certain criteria. Prices vary depending upon book category, but typical cost is around

$45.

- Available on Amazon.com.
- Free or on sale.
- A full-length book (minimum 125 pages).
- Not promoted by ENT in the past 90 days.

FACTORS THEY CONSIDER:

- Professional book cover.
- Positive Reader reviews.
- Book is professionally edited.
- How much the book is discounted (the larger the discount, the better your chances).
- Content of the book. Their website states, "We will not post erotica, pornography, books that contain controversial subject matter or books that may be considered offensive to any race, gender, religion, etc."

BOOK MARKETING TOOLS

BOOK MARKETING TOOLS is a website that instantly submits your Free Kindle ebook to 30 separate FREE Book Promotion sites with the click of one button.

Having invested many hours of effort submitting to individual sites, I think it's well worth the price ($29) to let Book Marketing Tools automate the submission process for you.

Please note: They will NOT be submitting your book to Paid Promotion sites such as those listed above – only to FREE book promotion sites.

TOP CHRISTIAN SITES

These sites are all operational as of this writing:

- Faithful Reads: HTTP://FAITHFULREADS.COM/AUTHORS/
- INSPIRED READS: HTTP://WWW.INSPIREDREADS.COM/

- Christian Book Readers: HTTPS://CHRISTIANBOOKREADERS.COM/
- Cross Reads: HTTP://CROSSREADS.COM/
- Christian Women Readers: HTTPS://CWWRITERS.COM/

Remember, this second phase of your Book Launch should come after you've garnered 25 positive reviews through the first phase, as described in Step 7.

On Day 91 after your initial book launch, assuming your book has been well-received and you have a minimum of 50 glowing reviews, you are ready to swing for the fence. And that can only mean one thing: BookBub.

BOOKBUB is King when it comes to online book marketing. They currently have more than 10 million active subscribers and completely dominate paid promotions.

BookBub is extremely competitive. They are rumored to reject 90% of all submissions. Having said that, it is possible. One of my self-published books, **The Special Blessings Prayer**, was accepted and featured upon first submission. It was featured for a second time six months later. Another of my self-published books, **God-Confidence**, was accepted upon second submission. So it can certainly happen.

If your book is chosen, you can expect to see thousands of downloads. Some books have even made it onto major bestseller lists thanks to BookBub.

In order to have a chance, you have to nail every aspect: the title, subtitle, cover design, internal design and content have to be stellar.

BookBub's website provides detailed information about making a submission for a Featured Deal. Prices range from $300 to $4,000 depending on your book's genre.

THE MINIMUM REQUIREMENTS ARE THAT YOUR BOOK MUST:

- Be discounted by 50% or more. (You don't need to discount your book prior to submitting it for consideration; they understand you can set the promotion for the agreed-upon date.)
- Not have been offered anywhere for a lower price in the last 90 days. (That means you can NOT have run a KDP Free Promotion within the prior 3 months)
- Be free of typos and grammatical

errors.

- Be on sale for a limited time.
- Meet BookBub's minimum page count. (Nonfiction books must be at least 100 pages.)
- Be available on at least one major retailer. BookBub prefers wider distribution. It is possible, although much harder, to be approved if your book is only on Amazon. If your book is only on Amazon, you will have a better chance if you offer it FREE to BookBub subscribers. With wider distribution, you can set it to $1.99 (or even $.99) to help recoup BookBub's rather hefty fees.

BOOKBUB'S QUALITY ASSESSMENT TEAM LOOKS AT:

- The number of authentic reviews on Amazon and Goodreads and their average rating.
- Whether the book has been positively reviewed by established publications or

prominent authors.

- Whether the author has previously written a bestselling book or received any noteworthy awards.
- The quality of the book cover.
- Whether the text is professionally formatted, and the product page is clear, informative, well-written, and error free.

Get started by joining BookBub and claiming your Author profile.

Be sure to follow me on BOOKBUB so you'll know whenever I have a new book or special promotion.

STEP 9: STAY ACTIVE ON SOCIAL MEDIA

Very few people like the idea of trying to "sell" their book. I certainly don't. And, well, that's sorta awkward when your goal is to become a best-SELL-ing author.

But what if there was a way to sell without seeming sales-y? Would you be on board with that?

YES. YES. And then right after that, here comes another YES?

If that's you, I've got some seriously good news.

There's one very simple way to sell your book without coming across as sales-y:

Involve people every step of the way, not just when your book is available for sale.

If you really want to be super-savvy, make the most of the weeks — and even months—leading up to your Book Launch. That way, you don't suddenly burst on the scene "selling" your book... and probably being ignored.

Instead, when you involve your social media following throughout your journey —during all the steps when you are <u>not</u>

"selling" your book—they will "buy in" to the book and be almost as excited as you are when it's finally released. There will be no need to sell it, they will go and grab it.

Plus, when you release your first book on Kindle, you're going to make it available for FREE to your social media following (as we covered in Step 7).

Talk about selling with no need to be sales-y! You're not even asking them to spend money. All you want them to do is click a link to download a free book.

Even for someone like me who doesn't like asking anyone for anything, that's pretty doable. Don't you think you can do it? Of course, you can. And you won't feel sales-y at all, I promise.

Now you may be thinking, "I already wrote my book. Too bad I didn't know this sooner." You can't turn back time, but as you refer to the following list, see if there are some elements you can still incorporate pre-Book Launch.

And of course, you can follow this strategy for your next book! You are planning another book, aren't you? I hope so, because that's exactly what we'll be covering in Step 10.

But first, check out all the ideas to help sell your book without being too sales-y!

12 GREAT EXCUSES TO TALK ABOUT YOUR BOOK WITHOUT SOUNDING SALES-Y

I learned the following absolutely brilliant strategy from Chandler Bolt, founder of the Self Publishing School.

Cool random fact: his brother is in my favorite Christian band, NEEDTOBREATHE. I may even have knocked over a bunch of people (in Jesus' name!) to get right up to the platform when they performed a concert at my church!

Social media isn't the place to sell. But it is the place to share your big news. And that's good news for you and your book. Because there are many perfectly newsworthy milestones along your journey that are well worth sharing.

Chandler Bolt came up with the following twelve, and I'm certain you can think of even more as you go along. Any time you go to a coffee shop to write...you can post a picture of it. If you go away to a beautiful location for a weekend to focus on writing, share all about it. Well, you get the idea.

Here are the 12 Newsworthy Milestones you should definitely share with your social media following. Let them know when you:

1. Decide to Write a Book.

2. Start Writing.
3. Finish Your First Chapter.
4. Finish Your Rough Draft.
5. Finish Editing the Book.
6. Run a Cover Design Competition.
7. Share the Results of the Cover Competition.
8. Pre-Release: Alert everyone about your upcoming FREE launch dates.
9. Launch Day:

Post to all of the forums and groups you've been actively engaging with, sharing that your book will be free today.

Stay engaged on your Facebook Profile and Facebook Group.

Post frequent updates with screenshots showing your book climbing the ranks within its category.

Host a Facebook LIVE, teaching the principles from your book.

Stay LIVE for at least an hour, urging everyone to go download the FREE book.

Consider hosting a webinar to invite people into your paid program. See Take Your Message to the World for the exact format you should use, including a script.

10. Launch Week Celebrations – report the results of your campaigns and share book reviews as they come in.

11. Launch Week "Thank You" – give shout-outs to everyone who supported your Book Launch.

12. Successful PR – If you get covered on websites or local media, share that as well. When

you run paid promotions, you can share screenshots and links to those websites, with your book featured alongside prominent authors.

STEP 10: WRITE ANOTHER BOOK, AMAZON LOVES SERIES

A mazon understands the most powerful management principle in the world: Behavior that gets rewarded gets repeated.

They want to sell more books. So they reward people who publish often.

That's why you should **Think SERIES**.

A Kindle book only needs to be about 11,000 words and solve one simple problem. When it comes to Amazon, you will be far more successful creating a 6-book series with a total of 66,000 words than you will publishing one book of 66,000 words.

Same amount of effort. Far more success.

That tip alone is probably worth the price of this book.

Speaking of this book, it is approximately 14,000 words. Has it provided more than enough information to be worth your investment of time and money? I'm feeling pretty confident the answer is a resounding YES.

This is one area where traditional and

self-publishing are completely different.

Good luck finding a traditional publisher to get behind your six mini-book strategy. It may change someday, but as of this writing, they will choose to print one 66,000-word book over six 11,000- word books every day of the week (except the Sabbath, of course). It just doesn't fit their business model for a wide variety of reasons which are beyond the scope of this book.

Why not re-evaluate your book to determine if you can publish it as a series of shorter books, rather than one long book? It's even more impressive to say you're the author of six books. Just make sure each book truly delivers value to the reader and can stand alone.

If you have enough material to divide the book into Three Parts (which is typical), you can almost certainly divide it into three Kindle books using the same natural division of material.

That's exactly what I did when I decided to share what I've learned during my thirty-year career as a Christian author.

Rather than writing one huge book – a format which doesn't even work well on Kindle – I thought about the natural divisions of topics that needed to be covered. And I came up with four distinct books covering various aspects of the process:

- Write Your Book in Just 30 Days
- Getting Started on Amazon KDP
- Successful Book Launch Secrets
- Balancing Ministry and Marketing

Then the first thing I did was have the covers designed on fiverr. Suddenly, the books were "real" – all I needed to do was fill the blank pages.

Can you think of a way to turn your current book project into a book series? I'm sure the answer is yes, so go have those covers designed on fiverr.com right away!

A nother great strategy is to plan ahead to do a substantial revision to the book (add two chapters, for example).

You can submit this revision to Amazon any time after your big promotion. They will email everyone who bought the book or downloaded it for free. And some who downloaded your book during the big initial promotion, but never opened it may be inspired to do so at this point.

It's also a great, free way to keep your name in front of book lovers. Anytime you can get a marketing giant like Amazon to work on your behalf, it's a major win.

You should be aware that Amazon staff will evaluate your book to make sure they consider the revision 'substantial' enough to qualify as a new edition. You will be required to submit an explanation of what updates you have made and why it's worth notifying those who already purchased the book.

CONCLUSION

Now you know the 10 Steps to a Successful Book Launch:

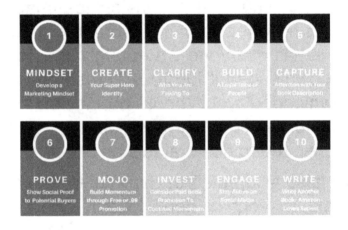

1. DEVELOP A MARKETING MINDSET – YOU ARE A MESSENGER!

2. CREATE YOUR SUPER HERO IDENTITY – YOU ARE UNIQUELY GIFTED!

3. CLARIFY WHO YOU ARE TALKING TO – YOU ARE A SERVANT!

4. BUILD A LOYAL TRIBE OF PEOPLE – YOU ARE AN INFLUENCER!

5. CAPTURE ATTENTION WITH YOUR BOOK DESCRIPTION – YOU BRING CLARITY!

6. SHOW SOCIAL PROOF TO POTENTIAL BUYERS – YOU INSTILL CONFIDENCE!

7. BUILD MOMENTUM THROUGH PROMOTIONS – YOU ARE A SEED SOWER!

8. CONSIDER PAID

PROMOTIONS – YOU ARE A WISE INVESTOR!

9. STAY ACTIVE ON SOCIAL MEDIA – YOU HAVE LOTS TO SHARE!

10. Write Another Book – You always have new ideas!

I hope you are excited about all the possibilities. People are waiting for the help and hope you can bring. Go out there and Launch Your book, reaching as many of them as you possibly can!

YOUR STEP BY STEP SUCCESSFUL BOOK LAUNCH PLAN

Okay, now that you understand the strategy behind a Successful Book Launch, here are the exact steps to follow:

PRE-LAUNCH & ONGOING

£   Follow Steps 1-5 to lay a firm foundation for your launch. Do not attempt your Book Launch without those key steps!

£   Build your social media following and your email list.

£   Do everything you can to make as many deposits as you can into those who can support your book launch.

£   Use non-sales-y strategies to generate pre-launch buzz.

£   Connect with influencers who might be willing to promote your free book offer to their circle of influence.

£   Create a Book Launch Team of supporters who receive an Advance Review Copy (ARC), in return for a commitment to buy and review your book the day it's posted. Set a goal of 100 supporters. You can gather them in a special Facebook Group and/or Messenger Thread.

ONE MONTH BEFORE

£   Set an official launch date.

£   Send your book to the three smartest people you know. Tell them your launch date and give them 72 hours to identify any errors in your book.

£   Make revisions and send out ARCs to influencers and your Book Launch Team. Tell them the launch date.

£   Create images and banners promoting your book release.

£   Plan & schedule a webinar or Facebook Live related to the book.

£   Generate anticipation on social media.

£   If you have a substantial email list or social media presence, prepare to offer a free class to all who can prove they purchased a paperback copy.

TWO WEEKS BEFORE

£   Contact all of your Influencers (those who received your ARCs or who have agreed to notify their circle of influence) to confirm your release date.

£   Confirm that your Book Launch Team members have their reviews ready to post and are prepared to buy the Kindle version at the regular price on Day 1, so they can post their reviews as a Verified Purchaser.

ONE WEEK BEFORE SOFT LAUNCH

£   Test your book layout using Kindle Viewer Software. Make any necessary corrections.

SOFT LAUNCH DAY

£   Upload your book to KDP <u>5-7 days before</u> the official launch date. Be sure to check your ebook on a variety of devices.

£   Call Amazon to add your book to 10 categories (Explained in great detail in **Getting Started on Amazon KDP**).

£   Have your key supporters buy the Kindle version at full price and post their reviews the next day. (Be sure they page through at least 25% of the Kindle version before posting.)

£   Log into KDP and schedule your first 3 Free Days.

DAYS BETWEEN SOFT LAUNCH & OFFICIAL LAUNCH

£ Keep asking until you have 10 positive reviews.

£ Implement any edits based on feedback from first readers.

£ Set up your Amazon Author Central Page.

£ Review the front of your book using the First Look feature. Make sure it looks great and that the hyperlinks work.

£ If you uploaded a paperback or Audible version, along with the Kindle version, be sure all three are linked together. This should be automatic, but if they are not linked within 72 hours, call Amazon for assistance.

OFFICIAL LAUNCH DAY

£ Notify your email list that your book is available FREE.

£ Be active on Social Media. Encourage everyone to download

the Kindle Version at the same time!

£   Host at least one Facebook Live. Promote the Free Kindle Version.

£   Share short clips to Instagram Stories.

£   Post your offer on all free book promotion sites and Facebook Groups.

£   Keep your Book Launch Team energized and promoting to their circle of influence.

£   Communicate with your influencers, sharing encouraging updates about the launch.

BOOK LAUNCH DAYS 2-3

£   Continue with the same activities as Day 1.

£   If you have a class related to the book prepared, host a webinar promoting your free class. Send them to purchase the **paperback** at the conclusion of the webinar.

POST LAUNCH

£   As soon as you have 25 reviews, schedule the other 2 Free Days within KDP for two weeks in the future.

£   Pursue Paid Promotions.

£   If you have not already launched a class related to your book, now is the time to do so.

£   Consider arranging a blog tour. There are companies who specialize in arranging them.

CPSIA information can be obtained
at www.ICGtesting.com
Printed in the USA
LVHW022033070423
743801LV00009B/188

9 781806 308170